This book
Ce livre

note to parents

Each French noun is provided with its word for **the** (**le**, **la** or **les**). It is important for children to learn this at the same time as the word.

pronunciation

All pronunciations are given in the word list at the back.

The letters **zh** are used to denote the sound that appears in the middle of the word **treasure**.

The **r** should not be sounded in the letters **er**.

Some long words have hyphens inserted to make reading easier. This has no effect on pronunciation.

written by Anne Hegerty
language consultant: John Williams
designed by Andrew Maddock

illustrated by Andrew Peters

Published in Great Britain by World International Publishing Ltd.,
an Egmont Company, Egmont House,
PO Box III, Great Ducie Street, Manchester M60 3BL.
Printed in Germany.
ISBN 0-7498-0779-2

A catalogue record for this book is available from the British Library.

Simple phrases

Here are some first phrases in French. See how the words **le**, **la**, **les**, **un**, **une** and **des** change the meaning.

le chat
the cat

un chat
a cat

la fleur
the flower

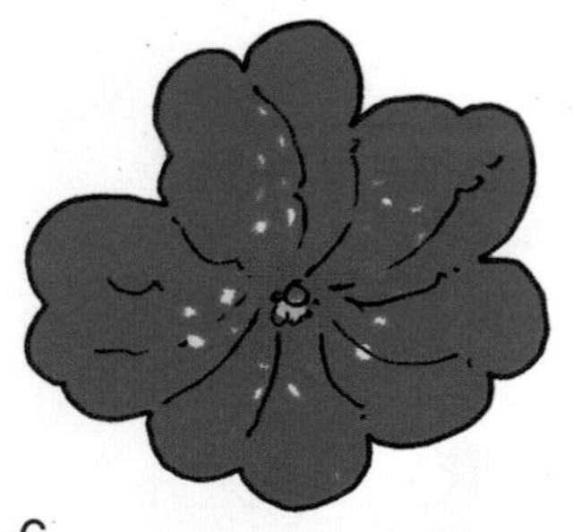

une fleur
a flower

les chats
the cats

des chats
some cats

les fleurs
the flowers

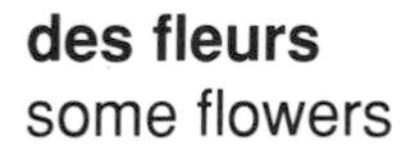

des fleurs
some flowers

Being polite

Here are some polite things to say.
Try them out on your friends.

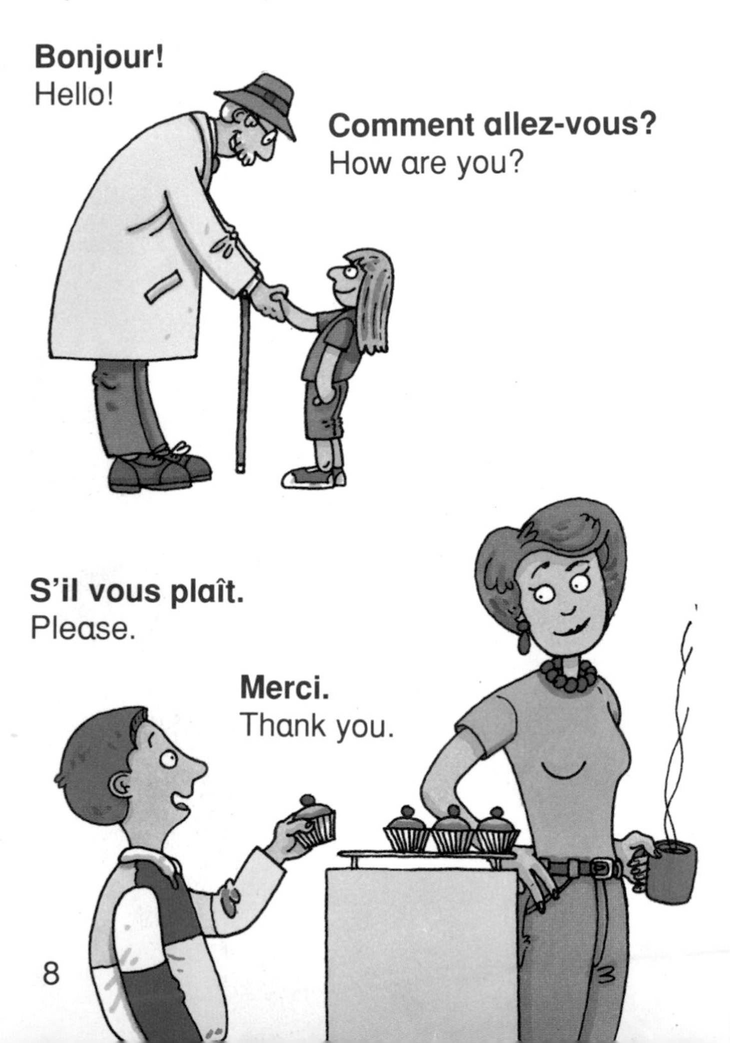

Bonjour!
Hello!

Comment allez-vous?
How are you?

S'il vous plaît.
Please.

Merci.
Thank you.

Excusez-moi.
Excuse me.

Au revoir!
Goodbye!

Who am I?

These French sentences describe who you are. Try saying them out loud. Which one describes you?

Je suis un garçon.
I am a boy.

Je suis une fillette.
I am a girl.

Nous sommes des enfants.
We are children.

C'est Maman.
It's Mummy.

C'est Papa.
It's Daddy.

What is your name?

With these French sentences you can tell your friends your name. You can ask them their names, too.

Comment t'appelles-tu?
What is your name?

Je m'appelle Marc.
My name is Mark.

Can you find your name in French? The little marks above some letters are called 'accents'.
Many French words have accents.

Christopher	**Christophe**	Emma	**Amélie**
John	**Jean**	Jane	**Jeanne**
Stephen	**Étienne**	Margaret	**Marguérite**

Je m'appelle Marie.
My name is Mary.

Counting to ten

These French sentences tell you how many things there are.
Look at the things around you.
Can you count them in French?

Voici quatre garçons
Here are four boys.

Voici sept chats.
Here are seven cats.

Here are the French names for numbers one to ten. Say them out loud two or three times. Then close the book and see how many you can remember.

one	**un**	six	**six**
two	**deux**	seven	**sept**
three	**trois**	eight	**huit**
four	**quatre**	nine	**neuf**
five	**cinq**	ten	**dix**

Il y a dix fleurs.
There are ten flowers.

How old are you?

With these French sentences you can tell your friends how old you are. Look on page 15 for other numbers to use. You can ask your friends how old they are, too.

Quel âge as-tu?
How old are you?

J'ai quatre ans.
I am four years old.

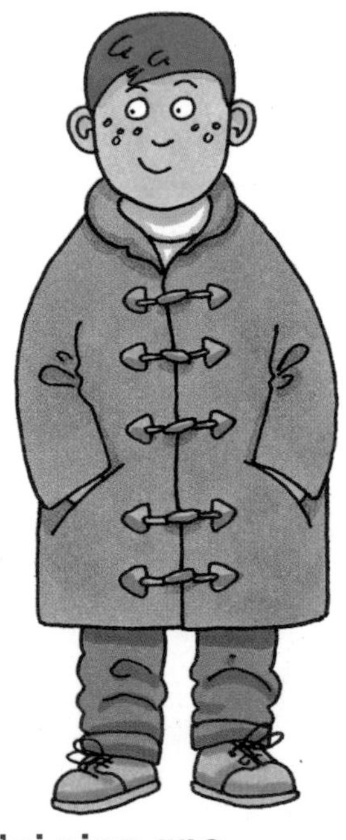

J'ai cinq ans.
I am five years old.

J'ai six ans.
I am six years old.

J'ai sept ans.
I am seven years old.

What time is it?

Here are some sentences that will help you tell the time in French.

Quelle heure est-il?
What time is it?

Il est dix heures et demie.
It is half past ten.

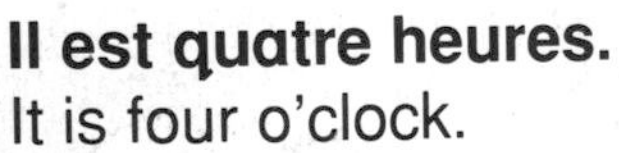

Il est quatre heures.
It is four o'clock.

Here are three French phrases for telling the time. Say them out loud two or three times. Then close the book and see if you can remember them.

et quart	means 'quarter past'
moins le quart	means 'quarter to'
et demie	means 'half past'

Il est deux heures et quart.
It is a quarter past two.

Il est six heures moins le quart.
It is a quarter to six.

What is this?

Here are some French sentences to help you say what things are.

Qu'est-ce que c'est?
What is this?

C'est la lune.
This is the moon.

Qu'est-ce que c'est?
What is this?

C'est un livre.
This is a book.

Qu'est-ce que c'est?
What is this?

C'est un chien.
This is a dog.

Qu'est-ce que c'est?
What is this?

C'est un jouet.
This is a toy.

Qu'est-ce que c'est?
What is this?

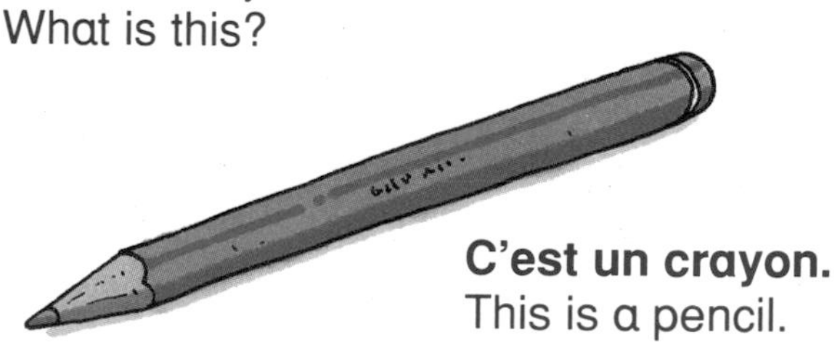

C'est un crayon.
This is a pencil.

My day

Here are some of the things you do every day. Which is your favourite? Say it out loud and try to remember it.

Je me lève.
I get up.

Je mange.
I eat.

Je vais à l'école.
I go to school.

Je joue dans le jardin.
I play in the garden.

Je prends un bain.
I have a bath.

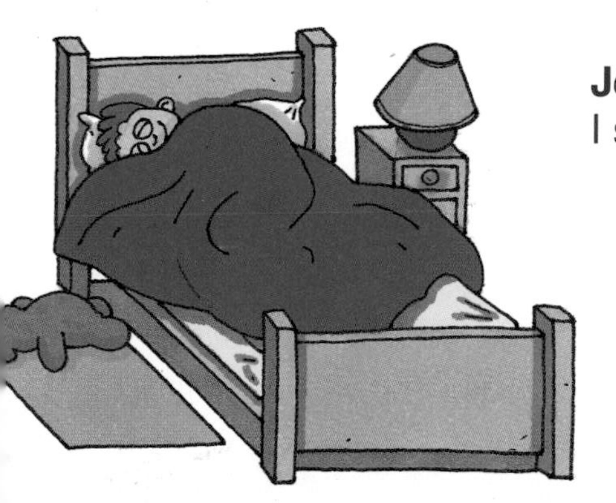

Je dors.
I sleep.

Where do you live?

With these sentences you can tell your friends where you live. You can ask them where they live, too. Try using the name of your own town in some of the sentences.

Où habites-tu?
Where do you live?

J'habite Londres.
I live in London.

J'habite près de Manchester.
I live near Manchester.

Habites-tu en ville?
Do you live in a town?

Non, j'habite à la campagne.
No, I live in the country.

Elle habite dans une maison.
She lives in a house.

What is it like?

These French sentences describe what things are like. Say them out loud.
Which do you have at home?

Le chat est noir.
The cat is black.

Le chien est blanc et noir.
The dog is white and black.

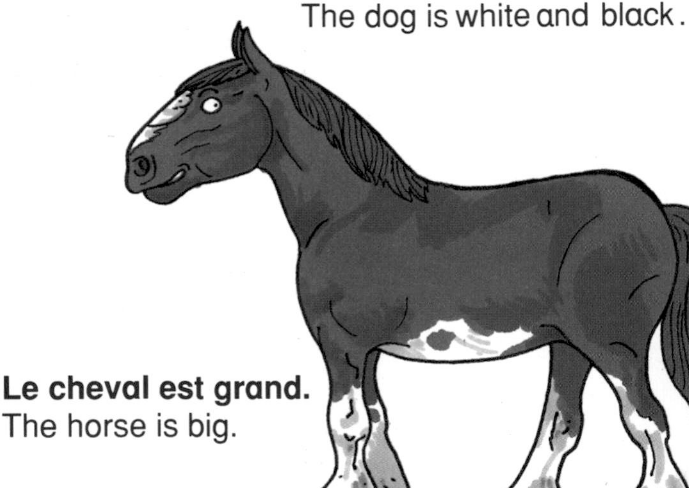

Le cheval est grand.
The horse is big.

Le bébé est petit.
The baby is small.

Le poisson est gros.
The fish is fat.

La saucisse est mince.
The sausage is thin.

What is the weather like?

Here are some sentences for talking about the weather. What kind of weather do you like the best?

Quel temps fait-il?
What is the weather like?

Il pleut.
It is raining.

Il fait beau, le soleil brille.
It is fine, the sun is shining.

Il neige.
It is snowing.

Il fait du vent.
It is windy.

Il fait du brouillard.
It is foggy.

Pronunciation guide

How do French words and phrases sound? Here are all the French words used in this book, with a guide to how they are said.

pages 6–7: Simple phrases

le chat	*ler shah*	**la fleur**	*la fler*

pages 8–9: Being polite

Au revoir!	*oh rer-vwah*
Bonjour!	*bonzhoor*
Comment allez-vous?	*commahn allay voo*
Excusez-moi	*exkewzay mwa*
Merci	*mair-see*
S'il vous plaît	*see voo play*

pages 10–11: Who am I?

C'est Maman	*say mamon*
C'est Papa	*say papa*
Je suis un garçon	*zher sweez ern garsson*
Je suis une fillette	*zher sweez ewn fee-yett*
Nous sommes des enfants	*noo som dayz ahnfong*

pages 12–13: What is your name?

Comment t'appelles-tu?	*common tappell tew*
Je m'appelle Marc	*zher mappell mark*
Je m'appelle Marie	*zher mappell maree*

Amélie	*amaylee*	**Jean**	*zhahn*
Christophe	*kristoff*	**Jeanne**	*zhan*
Étienne	*ett-yenn*	**Marguérite**	*mar-gay-reet*

pages 14–15: Counting to ten

Voici quatre garçons	*vwa-see katr garsong*
Voici sept chats	*vwa-see set sha*
Il y a dix fleurs	*eel ee a dee fler*

un	*ern*	**six**	*seess*
deux	*der*	**sept**	*set*
trois	*trwa*	**huit**	*weet*
quatre	*katr*	**neuf**	*nerf*
cinq	*sank*	**dix**	*deess*

pages 16–17: How old are you?

Quel âge as-tu?	*kel ahzh a tew*	**J'ai six ans**	*zhay seess ahn*
J'ai quatre ans	*zhay katr ahn*	**J'ai sept ans**	*zhay set ahn*
J'ai cinq ans	*zhay sank ahn*		